DANCING
INTO
THE LIGHT

AN INNER JOURNEY GUIDED BY
RUMI

TRANSLATIONS BY
OMID ARABIAN

ILLUSTRATIONS BY
SHILLA SHAKOORI

{ In Gratitude }

First and foremost, I offer gratitude to the spirit of Rumi, and to A.M.S. for opening my heart's eyes to this magnificent spirit.

This is the second collection of translations to come out of a course I have conducted since 2010, and so I am grateful to all who have attended and/or supported the course and shared their insights on these poems.

I am overjoyed that Shilla Shakoori has offered her marvelous drawings to illustrate this book, and I thank her sincerely for her kindness.

Always and forever I am indebted to Mojdeh for far more than can be enumerated here.

Last but by no means least, I offer gratitude to you, the reader, for taking this journey into the heart of all that is, with Rumi as your guide.

O.A.

POEMS

The poems that follow are selections from *Divan-e Shams-e Tabrizi* and *Masnavi*, the two major works of Jalaaleddin Mohammad Balkhi, known as Rumi (1207 - 1273 CE). The original source poem for each translation appears alongside.

While any act of translation inherently involves some degree of subjective interpretation, I have striven to keep as much as possible to the letter of Rumi's verses, not just to their spirit.

Readers are invited to delve into this collection with an open heart, and use Rumi's mystical poems as vehicles for their own inquiry into the great metaphysical questions of existence.

While the scope of each poem is by no means limited to one or two subjects, I have very loosely organized the selections in this volume by the following topics:

THE DIVINE HUMAN

{ 1 }

You are
an edition
of the divine book;
you are
a mirror,
reflecting the King's beauty.

Whatever is in this world
is not outside of you;
whatever you want,
seek it within yourself -
because you are it!

ای نسخه‌ی نامه‌ی الهی که توئی
وی آینه‌ی جمال شاهی که توئی

بیرون ز تو نیست هرچه در عالم هست
در خود بطلب هر آنچه خواهی که توئی

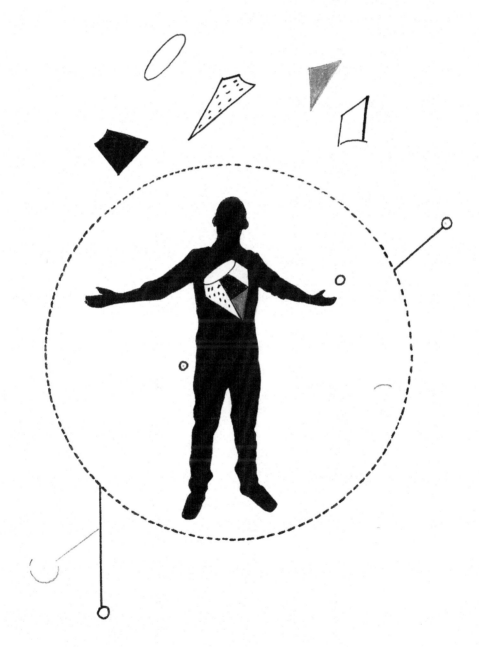

{ 2 }

You have the nature of God
when you enter into the heart:
the light of Mount Sinai
will radiate from within your chest.

You have the nature of light
when you enter a house at night:
the entire house will glow
from the brightness of that light.

You have the nature of wine
when you join any gathering:
from your beauty will arise
thousands of passions,
boundless fervor.

If joy has disappeared,
if desire has flown away,
when you let the water flow
oh, what flowers and plants will grow.

Even if the world is in sorrow,
if happiness has died away,
oh, what other worlds you can bring
from the unseen, into the seen.

This yearning within the restless
stems from you -
otherwise,
what could the dark mud know
of purity and clarity?

With one breath you weep
and with another, you till the soil -
but you are not a scavenger!
You are the mine,
you are the elixir.

{ Note: This is a segment of a longer poem. }

صفت خدای داری چو به سینه‌ای درآیی
لمعان طور سینا تو ز سینه وانمایی

صفت چراغ داری چو به خانه شب درآیی
همه خانه نور گیرد ز فروغ روشنایی

صفت شراب داری تو به مجلسی که باشی
دو هزار شور و فتنه فکنی ز خوش لقایی

چو طرب رمیده باشد چو هوس پریده باشد
چه گیاه و گل بروید چو تو خوش کنی سقایی

چو جهان فسرده باشد چو نشاط مرده باشد
چه جهان‌های دیگر که ز غیب برگشایی

ز تو است این تقاضا به درون بی‌قراران
و اگر نه تیره گل را به صفا چه آشنایی

نفسی سرشک ریزی نفسی تو خاک بیزی
نه قراضه جویی آخر همه کان و کیمیایی

{ 3 }

We live
by the grace
of that glorious light;
strangers,
yet deeply familiar.

Our ego is like a wolf;
but in secret,
we are grander
than Joseph in Egypt.

The moon
will abandon her vanity
if we
show our face to her.

The sun
will set fire to her lofty feathers
if we
spread our feathers and wings.

This human body is but a robe -
we are
that to which everyone prays;
we are
that before which everything bows.

Set your sights on the breath,
not on the body;
and let your heart be stolen
delicately,
tenderly.

The devil
saw only divisions,
and imagined
that we are separate from Truth,
separate from God.

Even Shams of Tabriz*
is but a pretext -
we are it!
We are the virtuous,
we are grace itself.

Tell the masses, as a guise
that *'He is the noble king,
and we are but beggars.'*

What do we need
from kings and beggars?
Joyously, we belong
with the true King!

By virtue of Shams,
we've disappeared;
beyond appearances
there is no He
and there is no Us.

---

*Shamseddin of Tabriz - 'Shams' for short - was Rumi's master and, for many years, his inseparable companion. The word 'Shams', rooted in Arabic, means 'sun'.

ما زنده به نور کبریاییم
بیگانه و سخت آشناییم

نفس است چو گرگ لیک در سر
بر یوسف مصر برفزاییم

مه توبه کند ز خویش بینی
گر ما رخ خود به مه نماییم

درسوزد پر و بال خورشید
چون ما پر و بال برگشاییم

این هیکل آدم است روپوش
ما قبله ی جمله سجده هاییم

آن دم بنگر مبین تو آدم
تا جانت به لطف دررباییم

ابلیس نظر جدا جدا داشت
پنداشت که ما ز حق جداییم

شمس تبریز خود بهانه است
ماییم به حسن لطف ماییم

با خلق بگو برای روپوش
کاو شاه کریم و ما گداییم

ما را چه ز شاهی و گدایی
شادیم که شاه را سزاییم

محویم به حسن شمس تبریز
در محو نه او بود نه ماییم

SPIRIT

{ 4 }

There is a spirit
- signless -
and we
are immersed in signs of it;
there is a spirit
- placeless -
and yet
head to toe
is its place.

Do you want to find it?
Then don't seek it
for a moment!
Do you want to know?
Then don't know it
for a moment!

When you seek it
in the unseen,
you are far away
from its evident self;
and when you seek it
in the seen,
you are veiled
from its hidden self.

But when you step out
of hidden and evident,
when you step out
of logic and deduction,
you can stretch your legs
and rest, happily,
in her protection,
in peace.

When you relinquish the road
a spirit will start to spring forth;
and then,
oh what grace will flow
from her essence,
from her flowing spirit.

You
who have imprisoned the spirit:
how long
will you pull back the reins?
Charge ahead,
hurtle it forward -
but not into this world.

Come out of greed,
take envy, and render it blind;
then stamp your feet
and celebrate -
for envy and greed
cannot speak of her.

How long will you run,
like the lowly,
for two loaves of bread?
How long,
for three loaves of bread
will you endure the spears?

روحیست بی‌نشان و ما غرقه در نشانش
روحیست بی‌مکان و سر تا قدم مکانش

خواهی که تا بیابی یك لحظه‌ای مجویش
خواهی که تا بدانی یك لحظه‌ای مدانش

چون در نهانش جویی دوری ز آشکارش
چون آشکار جویی محجوبی از نهانش

چون ز آشکار و پنهان بیرون شدی و برهان
پاها دراز کن خوش می‌خسب در امانش

چون تو ز ره بمانی جانی روانه گردد
وانگه چه رحمت آید از جان و از روانش

ای حبس کرده جان را تا کی کشی عنان را
درتاز درجهانش اما نه در جهانش

بی‌حرص کوب پایی از کوری حسد را
زیرا حسد نگوید از حرص ترجمانش

آخر ز بهر دو نان تا کی چو دوی چو دونان
و آخر ز بهر سه نان تا کی خوری سنانش

{ 5 }

The spirit is a vessel
that does what no other can:
it receives from the pure realm
and delivers unto the realm of soil.

Restlessly in love,
its work is to manifest;
it acquires from the heavenly throne
and pours onto the earth.

Once, it was not aware
of this realm, where it delivers -
if only it were aware, now,
of the realm where it receives!

From what spirits have bestowed
the land has become radiant
like a goldmine!
If only the soil had tongues
so it could speak of this...

So it could speak of the forest -
that eternal grove -
the one that feeds our spirit
secretly, invisibly...

In that forest
leopards and deer roar,
calling out to the divine -
to the one who tends to our sighs,
the one who draws us in.

A lion who feeds our self
with her own milk -
a lion who liberates
our selves from our selves...

A lion
who appears to us as a deer -
and in that guise,
lures us into the forest.

پیمانه ای است این جان پیمانه این چه داند
از پاک میپذیرد در خاک میرساند

در عشق بیقرارش بنمودنست کارش
از عرش میستاند بر فرش میفشاند

باری نبود آگه زین سو که میرساند
ای کاش آگهستی زان سو که میستاند

خاک از نثار جانها تابان شده چو کانها
کو خاک را زبانها تا نکته ای جهاند

تا دم زند ز بیشه زآن بیشه ی همیشه
کان بیشه جان ما را پنهان چه میچراند

آنجا پلنگ و آهو نعره زنان که یا هو
ای آه را پناه او ما را که میکشاند

شیری که خویش ما را جز شیر خویش ندهد
شیری که خویش ما را از خویش میرهاند

آن شیر خویش بر ما جلوه کند چو آهو
ما را به این فریب او تا بیشه میدواند

{ 6 }

If you find
the scent of spirit
emanating
from the hidden Beloved
- if you catch just one glimpse -
you will not be contained
in a hundred worlds.

When you accept
the seal of spirit,
you'll be king
without an army;
you'll conquer
the hidden realm,
and know what is unseen.

That treasure you've heard about -
the one you've chosen to dream of -
if you haven't found it on earth
you will find it in the sky.

If you are a guardian of love,
you will find
so much beauty -
effortlessly seen,
effortlessly yours.

In that blessed mirror
- clear, pure, and free of doubt -
you will find,
one by one,
signs of paradise
here in this very world.

Piereced by love's arrow,
intoxicated by the Beloved,
you may lose this life -
but you'll find
a hundred other lives.

The key
to the most intricate spells
will be effortlessly yours -
if you find
a moment's respite
from your whims and desires.

Shatter all the idols
on behalf of the King of life -
until you find,
in plain sight,
the one who gave form
to them all.

O Tabriz:
through Shams
- that light of truth -
you will find,
beyond doubt,
countless revelations
hidden in absolute mystery.

از دلبر نهانی گر بوی جان بیابی
در صد جهان نگنجی گر یك نشان بیابی

چون مهر جان پذیری بی‌لشکری امیری
هم ملك غیب گیری هم غیب دان بیابی

گنجی که تو شنیدی سودای آن گزیدی
گر در زمین ندیدی در آسمان بیابی

در عشق اگر امینی ای بس بتان چینی
هم رایگان ببینی هم رایگان بیابی

در آینه مبارك آن صاف صاف بی‌شك
نقش بهشت یك یك هم در جهان بیابی

چون تیر عشق خستت معشوق کرد مستت
گر جان بشد ز دستت صد همچنان بیابی

قفل طلسم مشکل سهلت شود به حاصل
گر از وساوس دل یك دم امان بیابی

درهم شکن بتان را از بهر شاه جان را
تا نقش بند آن را اندر عیان بیابی

تبریز در محقق از شمس ملت و حق
در رمزهای مطلق صد ترجمان بیابی

ORIGIN, BIRTH, DEATH

{ 7 }

Long before
there were grapes
and vineyards in this world,
our essence
was intoxicated
with that eternal wine.

Long before
all this commotion,
long before
Mansur made his declaration*
and headed for the gallows,
at the center of the world of spirit
in the divine city
we would proclaim:
I am Truth.

Long before
the one who is the Self of all
began to build
in the world of water and soil,
our joyous feast was under way
in the unbuilt tavern of truths.

Our spirit was as the universe
its cup was as the sun;
and by the grace of its wine
the world was basked in light,
up to its neck.

O wine-giver,
take these lofty ones
- so enamored with their water and soil -
and render them drunk;
so each one will realize
what a treasure he's left unheeded.

{ continued }

---

*Mansur Al-Hallaj was a 9th-C. Persian mystic who declared, 'I am the Truth.' He
was executed for heresy.

پیش از آن کاندر جهان باغ و می و انگور بود
از شراب لایزالی جان ما مخمور بود

ما به بغداد جهان جان اناالحق میزدیم
پیش از آن کاین دار و گیر و نکته‌ی منصور بود

پیش از آن کاین نفس کل در آب و گل معمار شد
در خرابات حقایق عیش ما معمور بود

جان ما همچون جهان بد جام جان چون آفتاب
از شراب جان جهان تا گردن اندر نور بود

ساقیا این معجبان آب و گل را مست کن
تا بداند هر یکی کاو از چه دولت دور بود

جان فدای ساقیی کز راه جان در میرسد
تا براندازد نقاب از هر چه آن مستور بود

ما دهانها باز مانده پیش آن ساقی کز او
خمرهای بی خمار و شهد بی زنبور بود

یا دهان ما بگیر ای ساقی ور نی فاش شد
آنچ در هفتم زمین چون گنجها گنجور بود

شهر تبریز ار خبر داری بگو آن عهد را
آن زمان کی شمس دین بی شمس دین مشهور بود

{ 7 cont. }

I'll give my life to the wine-giver
who arrives by way of the heart
so she can lift the masks
from all that is unseen.

Our mouths are open
in yearning and wonder
before that wine-giver who brings
casks of the wine that does not obscure,
honey without the bees.

O wine-giver:
close my mouth
or I will reveal
the treasure of the seventh realm -
the one that is the source of all treasures!

City of Tabriz,
speak, if you know;
speak of that time
when Shamseddin was exalted
without having been Shamseddin.

{ 8 }

I've come again, I've come again
I've come from the Beloved's side;
gaze onto me, gaze onto me --
I've come to shelter you from grief.

I've come in joy, completely free
from everyone and everything;
many thousands of years passed
before I could begin to speak.

I'm going there, I'm going there;
I was up high, so I ascend;
set me free, set me free again --
I've come transient to this terrain.

I was a bird of celestial air;
see how I took material form?
I didn't see her lure, and so,
swiftly I came, entwined in her.

I am the purest light, it's true;
and not a mere handful of soil;
I'm not the shell, for after all
I am the pearl, a royal gem.

Don't look at me with head-locked eyes;
look with your eyes of mystery;
come over there, then look at me -
for there I bear no heavy load.

I'm greater than the four mothers;
than seven fathers, greater still;
I was a jewel inside the mine,
I've come here to see and be seen.

My Beloved's come to market;
nimble and conscious, she has come --
why else would I have ventured here?
I've only come desiring her.

Shams of Tabriz, when will you gaze
upon the whole of creation?
For in this desert of decay
I've come to give my heart and soul.

{ ۸ }

بازآمدم بازآمدم از پیش آن یار آمدم
در من نِگر در من نِگر بهر تو غمخوار آمدم

شاد آمدم شاد آمدم از جمله آزاد آمدم
چندین هزاران سال شد تا من به گفتار آمدم

آن جا روم آن جا روم بالا بدم بالا روم
بازم رَهان بازم رَهان کاین جا به زِنهار آمدم

من مرغ لاهوتی بُدم دیدی که ناسوتی شدم
دامَش ندیدم ناگهان در وی گرفتار آمدم

من نور پاکم ای پسر نه مشت خاکم مختصر
آخر صدف من نیستم من دُرّ شَهوار آمدم

ما را به چشم سَر مَبین ما را به چشم سِر ببین
آن جا بیا ما را ببین کان جا سبکبار آمدم

از چار مادر برترم وز هفت آبا نیز هم
من گوهر کانی بُدَم کاین جا به دیدار آمدم

یارم به بازار آمدست چالاک و هشیار آمدست
ور نه به بازارم چه کار وی را طلبکار آمدم

ای شمس تبریزی نظر در کل عالم کی کنی
کاندر بیابان فنا جان و دل افگار آمدم

{ 9 }

On the day of my death
as my coffin passes by,
do not imagine
that I ache for this world.

Do not weep for me,
and don't cry out
"Alas, alas" -
you will fall
into the demon's trap
and that is cause
for true regret.

When you see my corpse,
do not speak of separation -
to me, that is the time
for meeting, for union.

When you entrust me to the grave,
do not say
"Goodbye, goodbye" -
for the grave is simply a veil
obscuring the crowds
just on the other side.

When you see me descend,
look for me to ascend -
when the sun descends,
when the moon descends,
do they suffer, is it a loss?

It may seem like setting to you,
but it is an arising -
when the grave becomes a prison
the spirit becomes free.

When a seed penetrates the earth
does it not sprout out?
Why then, do you have doubts
about the human seed?

{ continued }

به روز مرگ چو تابوت من روان باشد
گمان مبر که مرا درد این جهان باشد

برای من تو مَگریٰ و مگو دریغ دریغ
به دام دیو درُافتی دریغ آن باشد

جنازه‌ام چو ببینی مگو فراق فراق
مرا وصال و ملاقات آن زمان باشد

مرا به گور سپاری مگو وداع وداع
که گور پرده‌ی جمعیت جنان باشد

فروشدن چو بدیدی برآمدن بنگر
غروب شمس و قمر را چرا زیان باشد

تو را غروب نماید، ولی شروق بود
لَحَد چو حبس نماید خلاص جان باشد

کدام دانه فرورفت در زمین که نرست
چرا به دانه‌ی انسانت این گُمان باشد

کدام دَلْوْ فرورفت و پُر برون نامد
زِ چاهِ یوسف جان را چرا فَغان باشد

دهان چو بستی از این سوی آن طرف بگشا
که های هویِ تو در جو لامکان باشد

تو را چنین بنماید که من به خاك شدم
به زیرِ پایِ من این هفت آسمان باشد

{ 9 cont. }

When a pail enters the well
does it not come out full?
Why, then, would the Joseph* of spirit
cry out in fear
when entering the well?

When you close your mouth
on this side,
you can open it on the other -
your true voice rings out
in the atmosphere of no-place.

It may seem to you
that I have been buried -
but in truth,
I dwell
above all the seven skies.

---

*Joseph, son of Jacob, is a biblical character who was cast into a well and left to die by his own envious brothers. He was extracted from the well only to be sold into slavery, but eventually became the savior of Egypt during a time of famine.

REALITY, ILLUSION, TRUTH

{ 10 }

A Sufi entered a garden
seeking freedom and expansion;
he set his head upon his knees
as Sufis are known to do...

As he sank deeply into himself,
a meddlesome one passed by
and became distressed
by the Sufi's seeming slumber.

"Why do you sleep," he said?
"Awake, and gaze at the vines!
Behold these trees,
all these beautiful greens!

Listen to the Lord's command:
turn towards His creation,
and witness the evidence
of His grace!"*

The Sufi replied:
"O frivolous one,
all signs of Him are in the heart!
And what is outside?
Signs of signs,
nothing more.

The gardens, the meadows
are all within the spirit;
their reflection
forms the outside world,
just as an image falls
upon running water.

What falls upon the water
is an illusory garden
undulating
as the pure water moves.

But the groves
and the fruits
are within the heart -
it is their reflection
that falls upon
this water and mud.

If this world were not
an image of that heavenly cypress,
then God would not have called it
the realm of deception.**

All the deceived
have gathered round this image,
believing
- in error -
that here is the true grove.

They run away
from the gardens' source
and live a life of absurdity
built upon an illusion.

When they awaken
from this sleep of ignorance
they will see the truth
but what will it serve them
then?

Blessed are the ones
who die before their death -
for they have caught a scent
of the true source
of this vineyard."

---

*A reference to the Qur'an, Surat-ar-Rum, verse 50.
**A reference to the Qur'an, Surat-al-Hadid, verse 20.

{۱۰}

صوفیی در باغ از بهر گشاد
صوفیانه روی بر زانو نهاد

پس فرو رفت او به خود اندر نغول
شد ملول از صورت خوابش فضول

که چه خسپی آخر اندر رز نگر
این درختان بین و آثار و خضر

امر حق بشنو که گفتست انظروا
سوی این آثار رحمت آر رو

گفت آثارش دلست ای بوالهوس
آن برون آثار آثارست و بس

باغها و سبزه‌ها در عین جان
بر برون عکسش چو در آب روان

آن خیال باغ باشد اندر آب
که کند از لطف آب آن اضطراب

باغها و میوه‌ها اندر دلست
عکس لطف آن برین آب و گلست

گر نبودی عکس آن سرو سرور
پس نخواندی ایزدش دار الغرور

جمله مغروران برین عکس آمده
بر گمانی کاین بود جنت‌کده

می‌گریزند از اصول باغها
بر خیالی می‌کنند آن لاغها

چونک خواب غفلت آیدشان به سر
راست بینند و چه سودست آن نظر

ای خنک آن را که پیش از مرگ مرد
یعنی او از اصل این رز بوی برد

{ 11 }

Train your eyes on the wine-giver
and not on the one who drinks;
gaze upon Joseph
and not upon your hand.

You are life itself -
a fish in the net of body;
gaze upon the fisherman
and not upon the net.

Behold the essence
which you were at the start -
not the trifle
with which it is now adjoined.

Set your sights
on the endless meadow of flowers -
not on the thorn
scraping your foot.

Look at the regal bird
casting her shadow upon your head -
not at the crow
that leaps from your hand.

Grow upward
like the cypress and the hyacinth
and don't look down
like the violet does.

With the water of life
flowing in your channel,
don't look at the jug and the cask -
even if they break.

Grow towards the one
who gives life, and intoxicates -
don't moan about what is not
and don't focus on what is.

به ساقی درنگر در مست منگر
به یوسف درنگر در دست منگر

ایا ماهی جان در شست قالب
ببین صیاد را در شست منگر

بدان اصلی نگر کآغاز بودی
به فرعی کآن کنون پیوست منگر

بدان گلزار بی پایان نظر کن
بدین خاری که پایت خست منگر

همایی بین که سایه بر تو افکند
به زاغی کز کف تو جست منگر

چو سرو و سنبله بالاروش کن
بنفشه وار سوی پست منگر

چو در جویت روان شد آب حیوان
به خم و کوزه گر اشکست منگر

به هستی بخش و مستی بخش بگرو
منال از نیست و اندر هست منگر

قناعت بین که نرست و سبک رو
به طمع ماده ی آبست منگر

تو صافان بین که بر بالا دویدند
به دردی کآن به بن بنشست منگر

جهان پر بین ز صورتهای قدسی
بدان صورت که راهت بست منگر

به دام عشق مرغان شگرفند
به بومی که ز دامش رست منگر

به از تو ناطقی اندر کمین هست
در آن کاین لحظه خاموشست منگر

{ 11 cont. }

Look at contentment:
it is male, agile and spry -
don't gaze upon the female:
pregnant, and wanting.

See the ones who are pure
rising swiftly to the top -
don't gaze upon the residue
sinking to the bottom

Glimpse the heavenly faces
that fill the world,
and disregard the forms
that stand in your way.

In love's lure
there are strange and marvelous birds -
pay no heed the owl
who's abandoned the coop.

There is a hidden speaker
far more skilled than you;
so don't gaze upon the one
who is,
at this moment,
in silence.

{ 12 }

Visions of her are in your heart
so that you don't look here and there;
and she shows infinite grace
so that you won't come up
against any limits.

You'll take the seat of power
and dwell in abundance -
reside with Sufis of pure, vast vision -
if you set foot
outside this six-sided cloister.

You possess a door
- by nature invisible -
so don't search for doors
in the six directions;
a hidden door
through which you fly out
every night.

As you fly,
your feet are tethered
to an imaginary thread -
so that you don't fly out
once and for all -
so that at dawn,
you can be reeled back in ...

So that you will return
to this prison of a womb
until your creation is complete -
for this world is as a womb
and you are to be nurtured
by this blood.

When the spirit grows its wings
it will break through the body's egg;
it will fly out,
like the winged Ja'far*
and radiate its rays of gold.

---

*Ja'far ibn Abi Talib, a companion of Islam›s prophet Mohammad, lost his arms in battle and was said to have been awarded wings in their stead.

در دل خیالش زآن بود تا تو به هر سو ننگری
وآن لطف بی‌حد زآن کند تا هیچ از حد نگذری

با صوفیان صاف دین در وجد گردی همنشین
گر پای در بیرون نهی زین خانقاه شش دری

داری دری پنهان صفت شش در مجو و شش جهت
پنهان دری که هر شبی زآن در همی‌بیرون پری

چون می‌پری بر پای تو رشته خیالی بسته‌اند
تا واکشندت صبحدم تا برنپری یک سری

بازآ به زندان رحم تا خلقتت کامل شدن
هست این جهان همچون رحم این جمله خون زآن می‌خوری

جان را چو بررویید پر شد بیضه‌ی تن را شکست
جان جعفر طیار شد تا می‌نماید جعفری

LOVE

{ 13 }

This time,
I've become
entirely entwined in love;
this time,
I've cut off altogether
from well-being and comfort.

I have detached from myself -
now something else keeps me alive;
I've set fire at the root
to my thoughts,
to my mind,
to my desiring heart.

O everyone, o everyone,
I cannot be like all the rest!
What I've envisioned in my heart
would not cross
even a lunatic's mind!

The lunatic has shed his tears
and run away from the passion I feel -
I've mingled with the magnificent
and flown in the realm of non-being.

Today,
my mind has altogether abandoned me -
it keeps trying to frighten me,
imagining that I can't see!

But why
should I be frightened by the mind?
It's for the mind's sake
that I have taken form!
Why
should I be confused?
I have bewildered the one
who tries to bewilder me!

There's a purpose for which
I have stayed in this prison of a world -
why else would I be imprisoned?
I am not a thief!

{ continued }

این بار من یکبارگی در عاشقی پیچیده‌ام
این بار من یکبارگی از عافیت ببریده‌ام

دل را ز خود برکنده‌ام با چیز دیگر زنده‌ام
عقل و دل و اندیشه را از بیخ و بن سوزیده‌ام

ای مردمان ای مردمان از من نیاید مردمی
دیوانه هم نندیشد آن کاندر دل اندیشیده‌ام

دیوانه کوکب ریخته از شور من بگریخته
من با اجل آمیخته در نیستی پریده‌ام

امروز عقل من ز من یک بارگی بیزار شد
خواهد که ترساند مرا پنداشت من نادیده‌ام

من خود کجا ترسم از او شکلی بکردم بهر او
من گیج کی باشم ولی قاصد چنین گیجیده‌ام

من از برای مصلحت در حبس دنیا مانده‌ام
حبس از کجا من از کجا مال که را دزدیده‌ام

در حبس تن غرقم به خون وز اشک چشم هر حرون
دامان خون آلود را در خاک می مالیده‌ام

مانند طفلی در شکم من پرورش دارم ز خون
یک بار زاید آدمی من بارها زاییده‌ام

تو مست مست سرخوشی من مست بی‌سر سرخوشم
تو عاشق خندان لبی من بی‌دهان خندیده‌ام

من طرفه مرغم کز چمن با اشتهای خویشتن
بی‌دام و بی‌گیرنده‌ای اندر قفص خیزیده‌ام

زیرا قفص با دوستان خوشتر ز باغ و بوستان
بهر رضای یوسفان در چاه آرامیده‌ام

{ 13 cont. }

In the body's prison
I am immersed in blood;
it is for the sake of the unruly ones
that I have streaked my garment
with blood,
with soil.

Like a baby in the womb
I am being nurtured by blood!
Humans are born only once -
but I have been born
so many times!

You are drunk
and light-headed -
I am drunk and joyous
without a head!
You are smiling
and in love -
I am laughing
without a mouth!

I am that rare bird
who's left the garden
and leapt into this cage
- eagerly, willingly -
without a trap,
without a trapper

For this cage,
in the company of friends,
is far more joyous
than any garden,
than any field.
It is for the sake of the Josephs*
that I reside
within this well.

---

*See p. 34.

{ 14 }

Once again,
love pours forth
from my walls,
from my door;
once again,
my vengeful camel
has broken free from its binds.

Once again,
the lion of love
spreads its blood-streaked claws;
once again
my rabid heart
is thirsty for blood.

Once again
the new moon has arrived -
it's time for insanity!
All my knowledge
- alas -
how useless it has been!

Once again,
rebellion is born,
and a new army is formed;
once again
my sleepless Beloved
has severed me from sleep.

My dreams
have left me impatient,
my mind
has been washed away;
the Beloved
has lightened my load,
relieved me of my work -
now what is my task?

Rise up,
rise up again -
the uprising has arrived!
My fire, my passion,
fuels a hundred uprisings!

If Autumn has burned the garden,
like a lover's heart,
now my Beloved's face
is my garden, my meadow.

The worldly garden is scorched,
and the heart's garden
is illuminated;
this world's mysteries are burnt,
and my mysteries
are revealed.

O my caged body,
it's time to rejoice!
O my ailing heart,
the gift of wellness has arrived!

O wine-giver,
keeper of the tavern:
go and pawn my robes
- everything that I own -
in gratitude
for this gift.

{ ۱٤ }

باز فروریخت عشق از در و دیوار من
باز ببرید بند اشتر کین دار من

بار دگر شیر عشق پنجه‌ی خونین گشاد
تشنه‌ی خون گشت باز این دل سگسار من

باز سر ماه شد نوبت دیوانگی است
آه که سودی نکرد دانش بسیار من

بار دگر فتنه زاد جمره‌ی دیگر فتاد
خواب مرا بست باز دلبر بیدار من

صبر مرا خواب برد عقل مرا آب برد
بار مرا یار برد تا چه شود کار من

خیز دگربار خیز خیز که شد رستخیز
مایه‌ی صد رستخیز شور دگربار من

گر ز خزان گلستان چون دل عاشق بسوخت
نک رخ آن گلستان گلشن و گلزار من

باغ جهان سوخته باغ دل افروخته
سوخته اسرار باغ ساخته اسرار من

نوبت عشرت رسید ای تن محبوس من
خلعت صحت رسید ای دل بیمار من

پیر خرابات هین از جهت شکر این
رو گرو می بنه خرقه و دستار من

{ 15 }

Look and see
love
mingled with lovers;
look and see
the spirit
mingled with the dustbowl.

How long will you see
this and that,
good and bad?
Look and see, at last,
this and that
mingled together.

How long will you speak
of seen and unseen?
Look and see
the unseen
mingled with the seen.

How long will you speak
of this world and that world?
Look and see
that world
mingled with this world.

The heart is as the king:
it speaks,
and the tongue translates;
look and see
the king
mingled with the translator.

Come and mingle -
for it is for our sake
that the earth
has mingled with the heavens.

Look and see
water and fire,
earth and wind -
enemies, mingled as friends.

{ continued }

{ ۱۵ }

عشق بین با عاشقان آمیخته
روح بین با خاکدان آمیخته

چند بینی این و آن و نیك و بد
بنگر آخر این و آن آمیخته

چند گویی بی‌نشان و بانشان
بی‌نشان بین با نشان آمیخته

چند گویی این جهان و آن جهان
آن جهان بین وین جهان آمیخته

دل چو شاه آمد زبان چون ترجمان
شاه بین با ترجمان آمیخته

اندرآمیزید زیرا بهر ماست
این زمین با آسمان آمیخته

آب و آتش بین و خاك و باد را
دشمنان چون دوستان آمیخته

گرگ و میش و شیر و آهو چار ضد
از نهیب قهرمان آمیخته

گر چه کژبازند و ضدانند لیك
همچو تیرند و کمان آمیخته

آن چنان شاهی نگر کز لطف او
خار و گل در گلستان آمیخته

آن چنان ابری نگر کز فیض او
آب چندین ناودان آمیخته

اتحاد اندر اثر بین و بدان
نوبهار و مهرگان آمیخته

قند خا خاموش باش و حیف دان
قند و پند اندر دهان آمیخته

شمس تبریزی همی‌روید ز دل
کس نباشد آن چنان آمیخته

{ 15 cont. }

Wolf and ram,
lion and deer,
these adversaries
mingled together
in deference to the master.

Though they are tricksters and foes,
yet,
like bow and arrow
they are co-mingled.

Look and see
a King
by whose grace
flowers and thorns
mingle in the meadow.

Look and see
a cloud
by whose bounty
water from so many gutters
has intermingled.

Look and see
oneness
in its evidence,
and know
that Spring and Autumn
are joined together.

Fill your mouth with sugar
and fall silent;
find it a shame
for sugar and advice
to mingle in your mouth.

Shams of Tabriz
emanates from the heart;
there is no-one
as mingled
as he.

{ 16 }

How astounding,
when the sun enters Aries
in Autumn!
My blood has come to a boil
and dances in the body's rivers
a glorious dance!

Look upon this dance:
the waves of blood;
look upon the fields:
teeming with lunatics;
look and see
this unconditional joy
immune to the sword of time.

Corpses come to life;
old age becomes youth;
bronze becomes gold
while still in the mine -
in our city
everything transforms
for the better.

A city brimming with love
and elation;
every drunkard
holding a grand cup
in every direction,
raising a toast;
here, a river of milk
there, a river of honey!

Cities have one king,
but this strange city
is filled with kings!
The sky has one Moon,
but this sky
is filled with Moons, and Saturns.

Go,
go and tell the doctors:
you have no work there -
for in that place
there is no disease,
no-one can be harmed,
no disorder can be found.

No judges,
no policemen,
no ruler,
and no constables -
no-one keeping tabs.
How can conflict,
enmity,
and war
exist
upon the waters of the sea?

این بوالعجب کاندر خزان شد آفتاب اندر حمل
خونم به جوش آمد کند در جوی تن رقص الجمل

این رقص موج خون نگر صحرا پر از مجنون نگر
وین عشرت بی‌چون نگر ایمن ز شمشیر اجل

مردار جانی می‌شود پیری جوانی می‌شود
مس زر کانی می‌شود در شهر ما نعم البدل

شهری پر از عشق و فرح بر دست هر مستی قدح
این سوی نوش آن سوی صح این جوی شیر و آن عسل

در شهر یک سلطان بود وین شهر پرسلطان عجب
بر چرخ یک ماهست بس وین چرخ پرماه و زحل

رو رو طبیبان را بگو کآنجا شما را کار نیست
کان جا نباشد علتی وان جا نبیند کس خلل

نی قاضیی نی شحنه‌ای نی میر شهر و محتسب
بر آب دریا کی رود دعوی و خصمی و جدل

{ 17 }

For those who travel the path,
the mind is a chain -
break the chain,
and the way is clear.

The mind is a chain,
the heart's desires a deceit,
and this life a veil;
the path is hidden
behind these three.

When you rise up -
out of mind,
out of heart,
out of this life -
certainty arrives
amidst uncertainty.

A man is not a man
unless he's gone beyond himself -
love without pain
is but a fairy tale.

Make your chest a target
for the Beloved's arrows -
always in the bow
and ready to fly.

The heart that is stung
by her arrows
will have
a hundred targets in its sights.

Love is not
for the faint and the meek -
love is the work
of heroes and warriors.

Those who serve lovers
rule the world,
and hold all its fortune.

{ continued }

عقل بند ره روانست ای پسر
بند بشکن ره عیانست ای پسر

عقل بند و دل فریب و جان حجاب
راه از این هر سه نهانست ای پسر

چون ز عقل و جان و دل برخاستی
این یقین هم در گمانست ای پسر

مرد کاو از خود نرفت او مرد نیست
عشق بی درد افسانست ای پسر

سینه‌ی خود را هدف کن پیش دوست
هین که تیرش در کمانست ای پسر

سینه‌ای کز زخم تیرش خسته شد
در جبینش صد نشانست ای پسر

عشق کار نازکان نرم نیست
عشق کار پهلوانست ای پسر

هر کی او مر عاشقان را بنده شد
خسرو و صاحب قرانست ای پسر

عشق را از کس مپرس از عشق پرس
عشق ابر درفشانست ای پسر

ترجمانی منش محتاج نیست
عشق خود را ترجمانست ای پسر

گر روی بر آسمان هفتمین
عشق نیکونردبانست ای پسر

هر کجا که کاروانی میرود
عشق قبله کاروانست ای پسر

این جهان از عشق تا نفریبدت
کاین جهان از تو جهانست ای پسر

{ 17 cont. }

Don't ask people about love -
ask Love!
Love is a cloud
that rains down pearls.

It does not need me to explain -
love is its own explanation.

If you are headed
for the seventh sky,
Love is the proper ladder.

Wherever there's a caravan,
traveling,
it goes toward love.

This world
sparks out of you -
don't let it lure you away
from love.

Now close your mouth,
like a shell,
and fall silent;
for your tongue
is your mortal enemy.

Shams of Tabriz arrived
and life is filled with joy -
for he is one
with that eternal Sun.

{ ادامه ۱۷ }

هین دهان بربند و خامش چون صدف
کاین زبانت خصم جانست ای پسر

شمس تبریز آمد و جان شادمان
چونک با شمسش قرانست ای پسر

YEARNING

{ 18 }

Show your face -
I crave
meadows and gardens;
part your lips -
I crave
abundant sugar.

Light of virtue,
come out for a moment
from behind the clouds -
I crave
that radiant, glowing face.

I heard, once again,
the sound of drums
coming from your direction -
and so I returned
craving the King's embrace.

Coyly you said,
"Go, disturb me no more!"
I yearn to hear your voice
telling me again to go.

Bread and water
in this world
is like a flash-flood:
faithless, untrue;
I am a fish, I am a whale -
I crave the gulf,
the ocean's mouth.

This city, without you,
is a prison I swear -
I yearn to roam
in the mountains, in the deserts.

I am tired
of flimsy friends
and meek companions -
I yearn to be
with the warriors,
the lions of God.

{ continued }

بنمای رخ که باغ و گلستانم آرزوست
بگشای لب که قند فراوانم آرزوست

ای آفتاب حسن برون آ دمی ز ابر
کآن چهره‌ی مشعشع تابانم آرزوست

بشنیدم از هوای تو آواز طبل باز
باز آمدم که ساعد سلطانم آرزوست

گفتی ز ناز بیش مرنجان مرا برو
آن گفتنت که بیش مرنجانم آرزوست

این نان و آب چرخ چو سیل‌ست بی‌وفا
من ماهیم نهنگم عمانم آرزوست

والله که شهر بی‌تو مرا حبس می‌شود
آوارگی و کوه و بیابانم آرزوست

زین همرهان سست عناصر دلم گرفت
شیر خدا و رستم دستانم آرزوست

جانم ملول گشت ز فرعون و ظلم او
آن نور روی موسی عمرانم آرزوست

زین خلق پرشکایت گریان شدم ملول
آن های هوی و نعره‌ی مستانم آرزوست

یک دست جام باده و یک دست جعد یار
رقصی چنین میانه‌ی میدانم آرزوست

گویاترم ز بلبل اما ز رشک عام
مهرست بر دهانم و افغانم آرزوست

دی شیخ با چراغ همی‌گشت گرد شهر
کز دیو و دد ملولم و انسانم آرزوست

گفتند یافت می‌نشود جسته‌ایم ما
گفت آن که یافت می‌نشود آنم آرزوست

{ 18 cont. }

My soul
is weighed down
by the Pharaoh
and his tyranny -
I yearn to see
the shining face of Moses.

I am weary
of these weeping mobs
and their complaints -
I yearn
for uproar
and drunken howls!

One hand holding a cup of wine,
one hand caressing my Beloved's hair -
I yearn to dance
at the circle's center!

I can sing
better than a nightingale -
but because of these jealous hordes
my lips are sealed
while, all along,
I yearn to burst out in song.

Long ago,
a sage circled the town*
holding a lantern;
"I am tired
of these beasts and brutes!"
he said -
"I seek
a human being."

"We have all looked," they said,
"but none could be found."
"That's what I yearn for,"
he replied -
"the one who cannot be found."

---

*A reference to Diogenes of Sinope, the Greek philosopher who was often seen
carrying a lantern in daylight, searching for an honest man.

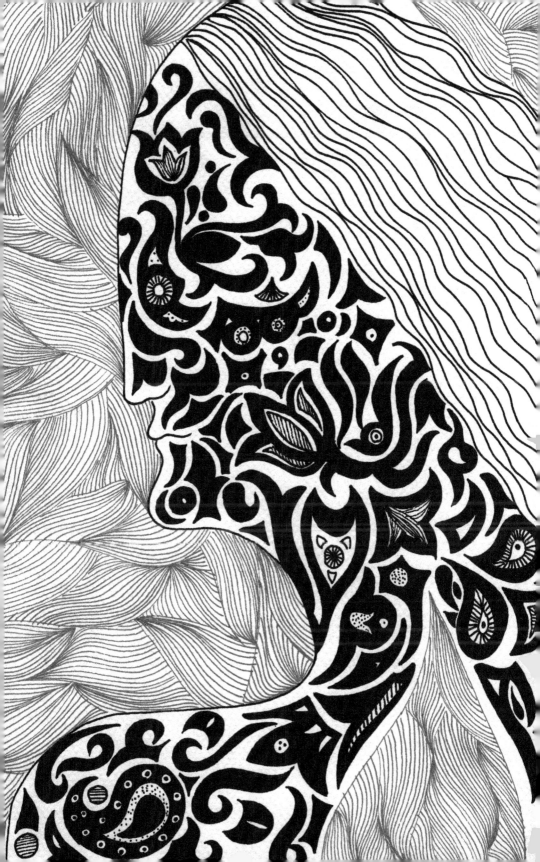

{ 19 }

I am ecstatic,
yet I want
to be more so;
I gaze into your drunken eyes
and say,
this is how I want to be.

I don't want a crown,
I don't want a throne;
I want to be
fallen on the ground
at your service.

My Beloved
took me by the throat
and said,
"What do you want?"
This, I answered –
just this, is what I want.

I want to breathe
the divine air;
but,
as I have my own breath,
I seek a grand companion -
a glorious confidant.

I am in the circle:
entering into the divine presence,
sheltered from all calamity;
I am as wax
searching for your ring,
yearning for your seal.

There is a different moon
hidden
in the heart of this moon;
I know this to be true, in fact,
but I want the certainty
that comes through vision.

بیخود شده‌ام لیکن بیخودتر از این خواهم
با چشم تو می گویم من مست چنین خواهم

من تاج نمی‌خواهم من تخت نمی‌خواهم
در خدمتت افتاده بر روی زمین خواهم

آن یار نکوی من بگرفت گلوی من
گفتا که چه می خواهی گفتم که همین خواهم

با باد صبا خواهم تا دم بزنم لیکن
چون من دم خود دارم همراز مهین خواهم

در حلقه‌ی میقاتم ایمن شده ز آفاتم
مومم ز پی ختمت زان نقش نگین خواهم

ماهی دگر است ای جان اندر دل مه پنهان
زین علم یقینستم آن عین یقین خواهم

{ 20 }

My task
is no task at all!
I am in love,
and in your love
there is no disgrace.

I've been captured
by the lion of your yearning;
and now, that lion
is my only prey.

What a rare pearl you are
within this ocean:
rendering me restless
like a wave.

I reside
at your ocean's shore;
drunk from your lips
though I have no-one to embrace.

I comfort my belly
with your wine -
the wine that leaves
no hunger, and no thirst.

Your wine
arrives for me from the sky,
and so
I don't have to beg and plead
with every common wine-maker.

Your wine
won't let mountains stay still -
so don't deride
if I've lost my dignity,
my gravity.

I conquer the world
like light from the sun -
without an army,
without a single horse.

{ continued }

کار من اینست که کاریم نیست
عاشقم از عشق تو عاریم نیست

تا که مرا شیر غمت صید کرد
جز که همین شیر شکاریم نیست

در تک این بحر چه خوش گوهری
که مثل موج قراریم نیست

بر لب بحر تو مقیمم مقیم
مست لبم گر چه کناریم نیست

وقف کنم اشکم خود بر میت
کز می تو هیچ خماریم نیست

می‌رسدم باده‌ی تو ز آسمان
منت هر شیره فشاریم نیست

باده‌ات از کوه سکونت برد
عیب مکن زان که وقاریم نیست

ملک جهان گیرم چون آفتاب
گر چه سپاهی و سواریم نیست

گر چه ندارم به جهان سروری
دردسر بیهده باریم نیست

بر سر کوی تو مرا خانه گیر
کز سر کوی تو گذاریم نیست

همچو شکر با گلت آمیختم
نیست عجب گر سر خاریم نیست

قطب جهانی همه را رو به توست
جز که به گرد تو دواریم نیست

{ 20 cont. }

And though I have no master
- no patron in this world -
neither am I weighed down
by useless woes and headaches.

So let me reside
along your street -
for there is nowhere else
for me to be.

Like sugar,
I've mingled with your rose;
it's no wonder then
that I am free of all thorns!

You are the axis of the universe -
everything faces you!
And so I will only
revolve around you.

My family
are those who are born of love;
for me
there is no more joyous tribe.

What is greater than both worlds?
The City of Love!
There is no better city for me;
no better land.

If I never write another word
after this,
it is not because
I don't have a beauty
to write about.

خویش من آنست که از عشق زاد
خوشتر از این خویش و تباریم نیست

چیست فزون از دو جهان شهر عشق
بهتر از این شهر و دیاریم نیست

گر نگارم سخنی بعد از این
نیست از آن رو که نگاریم نیست

HOPING,
TRUSTING,
ALLOWING

{ 21 }

Do not lose hope,
never despair -
for if today
the Beloved drives you away,
don't you know
that tomorrow
she will call you to herself?

If she closes the door to you
don't run away;
remain, patiently -
for on the other side of patience
she will seat you
at the highest seat.

And even if
she shuts all the roads
and all the passageways,
she'll show you
a hidden passage
unseen by anyone.

When a butcher
cuts off the ram's head
he doesn't discard his kill -
but picks it up
and carries it on his shoulder...

And when the ram's breath is all gone
he fills it up
with his own breath.*
Oh, where will the divine breath take you?
You will see,
you will see...

I say this only to illustrate;
but in truth,
her grace does not bring death to anyone -
but rather,
rescues all from death.

{ continued }

---

*Inflating the animal's carcass allowed for easier removal of the hide. Rumi cites
this ritual symbolically, to suggest re-animation through divine love.

هله نومید نباشی که تو را یار براند
گرت امروز براند نه که فردات بخواند

در اگر بر تو ببندد مرو و صبر کن آن جا
ز پس صبر تو را او به سر صدر نشاند

و اگر بر تو ببندد همه رهها و گذرها
ره پنهان بنماید که کس آن راه نداند

نه که قصاب به خنجر چو سر میش ببرد
نهلد کشته خود را کشد آن گاه کشاند

چو دم میش نماند ز دم خود کندش پر
تو ببینی دم یزدان به کجاهات رساند

به مثل گفتم این را و اگر نه کرم او
نکشد هیچ کسی را و ز کشتن برهاند

همگی ملک سلیمان به یکی مور ببخشد
بدهد هر دو جهان را و دلی را نرماند

دل من گرد جهان گشت و نیابید مثالش
به کی ماند به کی ماند به کی ماند به کی ماند

هله خاموش که بی گفت از این می همگان را
بچشاند بچشاند بچشاند بچشاند

She'll grant Solomon's kingdom
to an ant;
she'll gift both worlds
and never turn away a heart.

My heart circled round the world
and found not a single one like her!
Who is she like?
Who is she like?
Who is she like?
Who is she like?

Silence -
for without words,
she will bring a taste of this wine
- a taste of this wine -
to everyone.

{ 22 }

My sweet Beloved
shows no bitterness;
she never leaves my mouth
empty of wine.

Every dawn
she disrobes me -
"Approach," she says
"and I'll remove your cloak."

She surges into my house,
leaving me no respite;
she never ceases,
so how could I?

Her wine
has left my head spinning;
visions of her
have rendered my body
nothing but spirit.

Seven heavens
cannot contain her
and yet ... how does she travel
contained in my garments?

Feeding on her nectar
I am lion-hearted;
when she roars
I speak sweet words.

"You are in my grasp," she says
"I've created you -
you are my instrument
and so I shall play you,
caress you."

"I am your lyre," I say
"and when you strike me,
when you strum
each one of my veins,
I will yield, I will yield."

In short,
you will never
banish me from your heart;
and me -
I've lost my heart -
now what shall I do?

تلخی نکند شیرین ذقنم
خالی نکند از می دهنم

عریان کندم هر صبحدمی
گوید که بیا من جامه کنم

در خانه جهد مهلت ندهد
او بس نکند پس من چه کنم

از ساغر او گیج است سرم
از دیدن او جان است تنم

تنگ است بر او هر هفت فلك
چون می رود او در پیرهنم

از شیره ی او من شیردلم
در عربده اش شیرین سخنم

می گفت که تو در چنگ منی
من ساختمت چونت نزنم

من چنگ توام بر هر رگ من
تو زخمه زنی من تن تننم

حاصل تو ز من دل برنکنی
دل نیست مرا من خود چه کنم

{ 23 }

Little by little
the league of drunkards arrives;
little by little
the wine-worshippers arrive.

Softly, gently
the ones who caress the heart
are on their way;
beautiful as flowers
they arrive
from the meadow.

Little by little
from this world of *is* and *is not*
those who are not, leave;
and those who are, arrive.

Skirtfuls of gold,
each as vast as a mine,
arrive for the poor,
for those in need.

The weary and gaunt
return from love's pasture
healthy and stout.

The essence of the pure
like rays of the sun
arrives from high above
shining down.

Joyous is that garden
where, in the depth of winter,
fresh fruits arrive
for the holy mothers.

They are, in essence, grace
and the reflection of grace;
from one meadow to another
they arrive.

اندك اندك جمع مستان می‌رسند
اندك اندك می پرستان می‌رسند

دلنوازان نازنازان در ره اند
گلعذاران از گلستان می‌رسند

اندك اندك زین جهان هست و نیست
نیستان رفتند و هستان می‌رسند

جمله دامن‌های پرزر همچو كان
از برای تنگدستان می‌رسند

لاغران خسته از مرعای عشق
فربهان و تندرستان می‌رسند

جان پاكان چون شعاع آفتاب
از چنان بالا به پستان می‌رسند

خرم آن باغی كه بهر مریمان
میوه‌های نو زمستان می‌رسند

اصلشان لطفست و هم واگشت لطف
هم ز بستان سوی بستان می‌رسند

{ 24 }

Every moment
of each day
a new thought
enters your chest
like a dear guest.

A sorrowful thought
may steal away happiness,
but also serves it.

By sweeping the house
of what does not belong,
it makes way
for a new happiness
to appear from the source.

It shakes off
the yellow leaves
from the heart's branches
so green leaves can grow
in their stead.

It uproots old cheer
so new passion can enter
splendidly
from the beyond.

Sorrow weeds out
old, rotten roots
so new roots,
yet unseen,
can appear.

Whatever sorrow purges,
or takes out from the heart,
in its stead it brings
something better indeed.

This is true especially
for those who are certain of it -
for sorrow is the servant
of those who dwell in trust.

{ continued }

هر دمی فکری چو مهمان عزیز
آید اندر سینه‌ات هر روز نیز

فکر غم گر راه شادی می‌زند
کارسازیهای شادی می‌کند

خانه می‌روبد به تندی او ز غیر
تا در آید شادی نو ز اصل خیر

می‌فشاند برگ زرد از شاخ دل
تا بروید برگ سبز متصل

می‌کند بیخ سرور کهنه را
تا خرامد ذوق نو از ماورا

غم کند بیخ کژ پوسیده را
تا نماید بیخ رو پوشیده را

غم ز دل هر چه بریزد یا برد
در عوض حقا که بهتر آورد

خاصه آن را که یقینش باشد این
که بود غم بنده‌ی اهل یقین

گر ترش‌رویی نیارد ابر و برق
رز بسوزد از تبسم‌های شرق

فکر در سینه در آید نو به نو
خند خندان پیش او تو باز رو

{ 24 cont. }

If clouds and lightning
don't bring the sky to a frown,
the plants will die
of too many smiles from the sun.

Each time
a new thought
enters your chest,
go to greet it
with a smile,
with a laugh.

{ 25 }

Humans devise, and plot, and scheme
unaware of divine will -
but plotting and scheming
is nothing like divine will.

When the human thinks with his mind,
it's obvious what he'll envision;
he'll plot and scheme,
not knowing how to be God.

He'll take a step or two forward
as though he's going the right way;
but then, who knows
where he might be pulled!

Let go of the quarrel
and seek the Kingdom of Love -
for that kingdom will liberate you
from the angel of death.

Become a quarry unto the King,
and seek less your own prey -
for whatever you hunt
the hawk of time will take back.

Fall silent, and choose a place
where you will be at peace -
for whatever place you choose
the King will seat you there.

تدبیر کند بنده و تقدیر نداند
تدبیر به تقدیر خداوند چه ماند

بنده چو بیندیشد پیداست چه بیند
حیلت بکند لیك خدایی بنداند

گامی دو چنان آید کاو راست نهادست
وان گاه که داند که کجاهاش کشاند

استیزه مکن مملکت عشق طلب کن
کاین مملکتت از ملك الموت رهاند

شه را تو شکاری شو کم گیر شکاری
کاشکار تو را باز اجل بازستاند

خامش کن و بگزین تو یکی جای قراری
کان جا که گزینی ملك آن جات نشاند

بر نوشته هیچ بنویسد کسی
یا نهاله کارد اندر مغرسی

کاغذی جوید که آن بنوشته نیست
تخم کارد موضعی که کشته نیست

تو برادر موضع ناکشته باش
کاغذ اسپید نابنوشته باش

تا مشرف گردی از نون والقلم
تا بکارد در تو تخم آن ذوالکرم

{ 26 }

Who would write on something
that has been written upon?
Or plant a young tree
where another already grows?

She'll seek paper
that has not been marked;
she'll sow seeds
upon lands unsown.

You my brother,
be an unplanted field;
be a white sheet of paper,
unwritten upon...

So that your greatness
can be written upon you;
so that the divine
can plant seeds in you.

PURPOSE & ACTION

{ 27 }

Rise up, rise up,
for we are fellow warriors -
besides love,
besides love,
we have no other task,
no other mission.

In this soil, in this soil,
in this immaculate field,
we sow the seeds of love -
only love,
only kindness -
and nothing else.

How drunk we are,
how intoxicated
from that King who is us!
Come, come, let us get to work.

What did we drink?
What did we drink, that long-ago night,
that today, we are unquenchable drinkers -
always intoxicated,
and always wanting more!

Don't ask us, don't ask us
about the state of truth;
for we are wine-worshippers -
we do not count the cups!

You are not yet drunk -
you haven't feasted on that wine;
what do you know,
what do you know
of our hunt? of our prey?

We will not rest upon this soil
dormant and prone,
like so much straw!
We shall rise above this wheel -
for we are warriors
surrounding our foes.

بجوشید بجوشید که ما اهل شعاریم
بجز عشق بجز عشق دگر کار نداریم

در این خاک دراین خاک در این مزرعه‌ی پاک
بجز مهر بجز عشق دگر تخم نکاریم

چه مستیم چه مستیم از آن شاه که هستیم
بیایید بیایید که تا دست برآریم

چه دانیم چه دانیم که ما دوش چه خوردیم
که امروز همه روز خمیریم و خماریم

مپرسید مپرسید ز احوال حقیقت
که ما باده پرستیم نه پیمانه شماریم

شما مست نگشتید وزآن باده نخوردید
چه دانید چه دانید که ما در چه شکاریم

نیفتیم بر این خاک ستان ما نه حصیریم
برآییم بر این چرخ که ما مرد حصاریم

{ 28 }

How long
will you hold back
that laughter -
that glorious, dazzling moon?

Your true face
will make servants
of a hundred kings;
your laughter
will turn servants
into kings.

Teach the crimson rose
to laugh...
unveil
that eternal wealth.

The gates of the sky are shut
only to attract
a conqueror like you!

Trains of drunken camels
are watching,
waiting,
for someone to steer them!

Let down your hair,
and lure a hundred thieves
into your locks,
into the circle.

The day of union is here
and the Beloved is ready, present -
so don't even glance at the future.

The hard-faced drum
loves to be struck;
the reed
is yearning to be kissed,
dreaming...

{ continued }

چند نهان داری آن خنده را
آن مه تابنده‌ی فرخنده را

بنده کند روی تو صد شاه را
شاه کند خنده‌ی تو بنده را

خنده بیاموز گل سرخ را
جلوه کن آن دولت پاینده را

بسته بدانست در آسمان
تا بکشد چون تو گشاینده را

دیده‌ی قطار شترهای مست
منتظرانند کشاننده را

زلف برافشان و در آن حلقه کش
حلق دو صد حلقه ربابنده را

روز وصالست و صنم حاضرست
هیچ مپا مدت آینده را

عاشق زخمست دف سخت رو
میل لبست آن نی نالنده را

بر رخ دف چند طپانچه بزن
دم ده آن نای سگالنده را

ور به طمع ناله برآرد رباب
خوش بگشا آن کف بخشنده را

عیب مکن گر غزل ابتر بماند
نیست وفا خاطر پرنده را

{ 28 cont. }

So strike
the drum's face
and give breath
to the reed.

And if the lyre begins
to beckon and moan,
open your hand,
and caress it
generously.

If this poem remains imperfect,
don't deride -
my mind is unruly
and thoughts are fleeting.

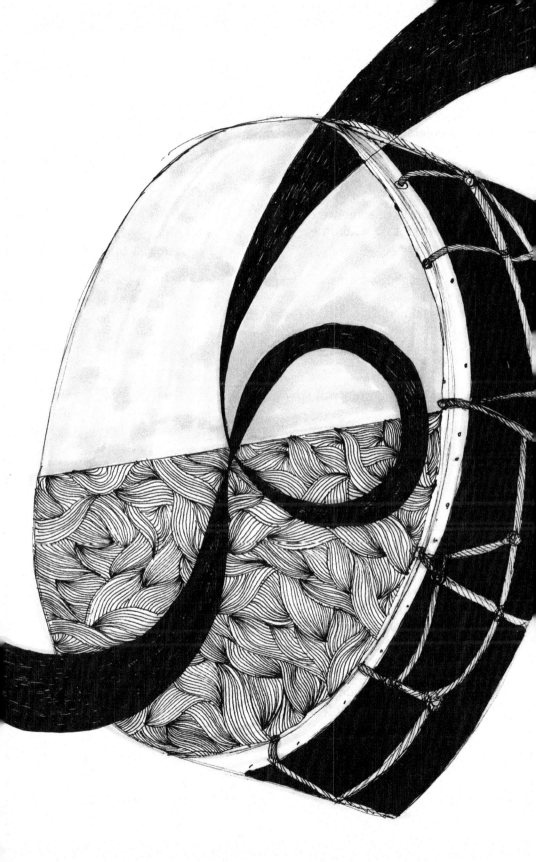

{ 29 }

I set a new fire
to my being,
and entered
a new non-being,
a new void.

Good and bad exist
in the world of existence -
but I am not good, brother,
nor am I bad.

Like the night watchman
I prowled
and reclaimed
from the thieving wheel
what it had taken from me.

I was a solitary one
with a hundred pompous selves;
now,
the solitary one is gone
– no trace of it left -
and I am a hundred -
I am the all.

One cannot come this way
without surpassing the self;
I left that self behind,
then came on my way.

My stature was dwarfed
by the stature of Love;
when my grandness became vile,
then I became grand.

I learned from the divine
the craft of being human;
now I am Love's champion,
joined with the divine.

Twenty-nine letters
on the tablet of life;
I've cleared off all the letters,
all the words,
and gone back to the start.

Shams of Tabriz
shone like a star,
and in his presence
my fortune, too, is bright.

آتشی نو در وجود اندرزدیم
در میان محو نو اندرشدیم

نیك و بد اندر جهان هستی است
ما نه نیكیم ای برادر نی بدیم

هر چه چرخ دزد از ما برده بود
شب عسس رفتیم و از وی بستدیم

ما یکی بودیم با صد ما و من
یك جوی زان یك نماند و ما صدیم

از خودی نارفته نتوان آمدن
از خودی رفتیم وانگه آمدیم

قد ما شد پست اندر قد عشق
قد ما چون پست شد عالی قدیم

پیشه‌ی مردی ز حق آموختیم
پهلوان عشق و یار احمدیم

بیست و نه حرف است بر لوح وجود
حرف‌ها شستیم و اندر ابجدیم

سعد شمس الدین تبریزی بتافت
وز قران سعد او ما اسعدیم

JOY

I have made a pact with joy
for joy to be forever mine;
I've made a pledge
with Life of Life
for her to remain my Beloved.

The great Ruler
has given me a decree
written by her own hand:
that she shall be the one I serve
for as long as there's a throne.

Whether I am sober
or completely drunk,
no-one else W
will take my hand and guide;
and if I should injure my hand
she will be my healer, too.

Idle thoughts do not dare
circle around my city walls -
who can transgress my borders
while she is my emperor?

By the grace of her ruby lips
my face is never pale;
even Rostam* will fall before me
for she is my warrior.

I will strike fear in Venus
and graze the face of the moon;
I will conquer the heavens
for she is my Saturn.

I illuminate the world
as long as I receive the sun;
I rule the mallet and the ball
when the heart is my arena.

I am Egypt, immersed in sugar
holding Joseph** in my arms -
what land of plenty do I seek?
She is my promised land!

Guardian,
keeper,
liberator...
she is ever-present
and self-evident proof
for me
and for all who deny.

There is a spirit in the world
that shuns all form -
and yet,
she takes human shape
and becomes
my humanity.

---

*Rostam is the foremost hero of Ferdowsi's epic poem *Shahnameh* (10th C. CE).
**See p. 34

مرا عهدیست با شادی که شادی آن من باشد
مرا قولیست با جانان که جانان جان من باشد

به خط خویشتن فرمان به دستم داد آن سلطان
که تا تختست و تا بختست او سلطان من باشد

اگر هشیار اگر مستم نگیرد غیر او دستم
وگر من دست خود خستم هم او درمان من باشد

چه زهره دارد اندیشه که گرد شهر من گردد
که قصد ملک من دارد چو او خاقان من باشد

نبیند روی من زردی به اقبال لب لعلش
بمیرد پیش من رستم چو او دستان من باشد

بدرم زهرهی زهره خراشم ماه را چهره
برم از آسمان مهره چو او کیوان من باشد

چراغ چرخ گردونم چو اجری خوار خورشیدم
امیر گوی و چوگانم چو دل میدان من باشد

منم مصر و شکرخانه چو یوسف در برم گیرم
چه جویم ملک کنعان را چو او کنعان من باشد

زهی حاضر زهی ناظر زهی حافظ زهی ناصر
زهی الزام هر منکر چو او برهان من باشد

یکی جانیست در عالم که ننگش آید از صورت
بپوشد صورت انسان ولی انسان من باشد

{ 31 }

O lovers,
every moment
a toast:
to your joyous revelries -
may you turn this world
into a sugar mine!

O lovers,
your drunken dance
has reached the great throne;
this lovers' caravan
has left the earth
and surpassed the heavens.

O lovers,
how can I speak
of the ocean's shore,
when the ocean of life
has no shores at all!
It is greater than place
and greater than no-place.

O lovers,
like waves we rise up,
and bow down in worship -
so that the unseen
can become seen.

O lovers,
if someone asks,
who are you warriors
answer them thus:
we are the life
of life
of life.

O lovers,
the ocean of life
is giving and generous -
always gifting priceless gems
even to those
who are not divers.

{ continued }

عیشهاتان نوش بادا هر زمان ای عاشقان
وز شما کان شکر باد این جهان ای عاشقان

نوش و جوش عاشقان تا عرش و تا کرسی رسید
برگذشت از عرش و فرش این کاروان ای عاشقان

از لب دریا چه گویم لب ندارد بحر جان
برفزودست از مکان و لامکان ای عاشقان

ما مثال موجها اندر قیام و در سجود
تا بدید آید نشان از بی نشان ای عاشقان

گر کسی پرسد کیانید ای سراندازان شما
هین بگوییدش که جان جان جان ای عاشقان

گر کسی غواص نبود بحر جان بخشنده است
کاو همی بخشد گهرها رایگان ای عاشقان

زیر پای من گل است و زیر پاهاشان گل است
چون بکوبم پا میان منکران ای عاشقان

خرما آن دم که از مستی جانان جان ما
می نداند آسمان از ریسمان ای عاشقان

طرفه دریایی معلق آمد این دریای عشق
نی به زیر و نی به بالا نی میان ای عاشقان

تا بدید آمد شعاع شمس تبریزی ز شرق
جان مطلق شد زمین و آسمان ای عاشقان

O lovers,
with this event
and that event
the masses were swindled -
but we became free
once again
from this and from that.

O lovers,
beneath my feet
there are flowers,
and beneath theirs
there is mud -
this is how I dance
and stomp my feet
among the deniers,
surrounded by cynics.

O lovers,
how blissful, that moment
when
drunk with the beloved,
our spirit does not know
up from down,
this from that.

O lovers,
this ocean of love
is a wonder indeed
neither below
nor above
and not in between -
but suspended
and afloat.

O lovers,
when rays of Shams
appear from the East,
heaven and earth become
nothing but spirit...
pure,
free,
untethered spirit.

I am a servant of the Moon -
so speak only of the Moon!
Speak to me of candlelight,
of sweetness,
and of nothing else.

Speak not of suffering,
only of treasure -
and if this is not known to you,
suffer not,
and speak not.

Last night,
as I roared in madness,
Love saw me, and said:
I'm here,
no need to wail
or tear your garments -
just say nothing.

I said:
O love,
there is something else I fear.

Love said:
That something else
does not exist -
say no more.

I will whisper in your ear
mysterious words;
just nod your head
in consent,
and beyond that gesture
say no more.

On the heart's journey
upon love's path,
a beauty came into view -
as though life itself
had appeared...
Oh how sweet this journey!
How exquisite!

I asked my heart:
Who is this beauty?
My heart replied
with a gesture:
It's beyond your grasp,
greater than you can fathom -
so say nothing, and travel on.

Awestruck, I asked,
Is it an angel's face?
Or a human being's?

Hush, replied my heart,
it is beyond human,
and beyond angel.

What is it then?
Tell me, I begged,
I am in a frenzy!

Stay in this state,
my heart replied,
and say nothing.

You dwell in a house
of fantasies and illusion!
Arise,
pack your bags,
leave this house,
and say no more.

O heart, I said,
speak as a father would -
is this not a tale of God?

Yes,
my heart replied,
but swear on your father's life
that you will say no more!

من غلام قمرم غیر قمر هیچ مگو
پیش من جز سخن شمع و شکر هیچ مگو

سخن رنج مگو جز سخن گنج مگو
ور از این بی‌خبری رنج مبر هیچ مگو

دوش دیوانه شدم عشق مرا دید و بگفت
آمدم نعره مزن جامه مدر هیچ مگو

گفتم ای عشق من از چیز دگر می‌ترسم
گفت آن چیز دگر نیست دگر هیچ مگو

من به گوش تو سخن‌های نهان خواهم گفت
سر بجنبان که بلی جز که به سر هیچ مگو

قمری جان صفتی در ره دل پیدا شد
در ره دل چه لطیف است سفر هیچ مگو

گفتم ای دل چه مه‌ست این دل اشارت می‌کرد
که نه اندازه‌ی توست این بگذر هیچ مگو

گفتم این روی فرشته‌ست عجب یا بشر است
گفت این غیر فرشته‌ست و بشر هیچ مگو

گفتم این چیست بگو زیر و زبر خواهم شد
گفت می‌باش چنین زیر و زبر هیچ مگو

ای نشسته تو در این خانه‌ی پرنقش و خیال
خیز از این خانه برو رخت ببر هیچ مگو

گفتم ای دل پدری کن نه که این وصف خداست
گفت این هست ولی جان پدر هیچ مگو

UNION

{ 33 }

With each breath
love's call arrives
from every direction,
left and right;
we are headed for the sky
but who is going to see whom?

We've resided in the sky,
companions of angels;
once again, we journey there
for that is our native land.

We are higher than the sky,
we are greater than angels -
then why not surpass them both?
Our home is the divine throne!

What is the world of soil
compared to the pure essence?
Where have you landed?
What is this place?
Pack your bags!

New fortune is on our side;
our task is to give our life;
divine light,
the pride of the universe
is leading our caravan.

This gentle breeze
bears the scent of her locks;
my brilliant visions
emanate
from her dazzling face.

Look into this heart of ours:
every moment, a miracle!
In spite of this spectacle,
your eyes are looking elsewhere -
why?

{ continued }

هر نفس آواز عشق می‌رسد از چپ و راست
ما به فلك می‌رویم عزم تماشا كراست

ما به فلك بوده‌ایم یار ملك بوده‌ایم
باز همان جا رویم جمله كه آن شهر ماست

خود ز فلك برتریم وز ملك افزونتریم
زین دو چرا نگذریم منزل ما كبریاست

گوهر پاك از كجا عالم خاك از كجا
بر چه فرود آمدیت بار كنید این چه جاست

بخت جوان یار ما دادن جان كار ما
قافله سالار ما فخر جهان مصطفاست

بوی خوش این نسیم از شكن زلف اوست
شعشعه‌ی این خیال زان رخ چون والضحاست

در دل ما درنگر هر دم شق قمر
كز نظر آن نظر چشم تو آن سو چراست

خلق چو مرغابیان زاده ز دریای جان
كی كند این جا مقام مرغ كز آن بحر خاست

بلك به دریا دریم جمله در او حاضریم
ور نه ز دریای دل موج پیاپی چراست

آمد موج الست كشتی قالب ببست
باز چو كشتی شكست نوبت وصل و لقاست

{ 33 cont. }

Humans are like water-fowl:
born from the ocean of life -
why would a bird make its nest here
when it has arisen from that sea?

No, we are in the ocean,
all of us present within her -
if not, then why
do waves continually arise
from the ocean of the heart?

Now,
that primordial wave has come,
headed for this vessel,
this body,
this ship;
once again,
when the ship is shattered,
it's time for union
face to face.

{ 34 }

It's time for union,
face-to-face;
it's time for uprising,
for immortality;
it's time for tenderness
and benevolence;
the sea of light
is luminous and undimmed.

A royal decree has appeared
proclaiming abundance,
urging generosity;
the ocean's roar
can be heard;
good fortune has dawned,
but it is not merely morning -
it is the light of the divine.

What are these images?
Whose are these faces?
Who is this King, this ruler,
this ancient consciousness?
There are so many veils!

The cure for the veils
is upheavals like this!
The wellspring of these waters
is in your head, is in your eyes.

Twist around in your head,
but know
that you have two heads:
an earthly one,
made of soil,
and a pure one,
from the heavens.

So many pure heads
have fallen to the ground
so that you may know
that this head exists
by virtue of the other head.

The true, essential head is hidden,
and this minor one evident;
but know,
that behind this world
is another, infinite realm.

Now lid the cask
o water-bearer,
our water-jugs can take no more -
our perceptions are constricted
living in this constricted world.

Out from Tabriz shone Shams
- the Light of Truth -
and to him I said:
your light is joined
with everyone,
and at the same time
singular.

نوبت وصل و لقاست نوبت حشر و بقاست
نوبت لطف و عطاست بحر صفا در صفاست

درج عطا شد پدید غرهی دریا رسید
صبح سعادت دمید صبح چه نور خداست

صورت و تصویر کیست این شه و این میر کیست
این خرد پیر کیست این همه روپوشهاست

چارهی روپوشها هست چنین جوشها
چشمهی این نوشها در سر و چشم شماست

در سر خود پیچ لیك هست شما را دو سر
این سر خاك از زمین وان سر پاك از سماست

ای بس سرهای پاك ریخته در پای خاك
تا تو بدانی که سر زان سر دیگر به پاست

آن سر اصلی نهان وآن سر فرعی عیان
دانك پس این جهان عالم بیمنتهاست

مشك ببند ای سقا مینبرد خنب ما
کوزهی ادراكها تنگ از این تنگناست

از سوی تبریز تافت شمس حق و گفتمش
نور تو هم متصل با همه و هم جداست

{ 35 }

With each breath, love's call arrives
from every direction, left and right;
we are headed for the fields,
but who is going to see whom?

The time for houses has passed –
the time for meadows is here;
prosperity has dawned, and now
it's time for union, face to face.

O blessed king, arise, arise,
awake from your heavy sleep;
ride, ride upon fortune's horse –
it's time for us to conjoin.

Hear the drums, recall your oath;
the way to the sky is swept clean;
your joy is the currency –
no sign of tomorrow's debts.

Light has lifted up its hands,
and shattered the dark of night;
the whole world, above and below
is full of clarity and radiance.

How blissful are the ones unbound
by these colors and these scents –
for there are, beyond all this,
so many colors in the heart.

How blessed that heart, that spirit
who becomes free from water and mud –
though within this water and mud
lies the means for alchemy.

هر نفس آواز عشق می رسد از چپ و راست
ما به چمن می رویم عزم تماشا کراست

نوبت خانه گذشت نوبت بستان رسید
صبح سعادت دمید وقت وصال و لقاست

ای شه صاحب قران خیز ز خواب گران
مرکب دولت بران نوبت وصل آن ماست

طبل وفا کوفتند راه سما روفتند
عیش شما نقد شد نسیه‌ی فردا کجاست

روم برآورد دست زنگی شب را شکست
عالم بالا و پست پرلمعان و صفاست

ای خنک آن را که او رست از این رنگ و بو
زانک جز این رنگ و بو در دل و جان رنگ هاست

ای خنک آن جان و دل کو رهد از آب و گل
گر چه در این آب و گل دستگه کیمیاست

{ 36 }

Sprinkle water upon the road* -
the Beloved arrives!
Bring the garden this good news:
the scent of Spring arrives!

Clear the way for her -
that enchanting full moon;
for it's from her dazzling face
that our light arrives.

The sky is torn asunder;
there's a rumbling in the world;
the scent of ambergris and musk is in the air;
the Beloved's banner arrives.

The splendor of the garden arrives;
the eyes, and the light of the eyes, arrives;
sorrow steps aside,
and beauty arrives at our side.

The arrows fly effortlessly
and sail towards the target -
then why are we sitting back?
The King arrives at the hunt!

The garden salutes,
and the cypress rises up;
the blades of grass march ahead,
and the flowerbuds arrive
riding on their stems.

The sky-dwellers drink and drink
until the spirit is intoxicated,
and even the intellect arrives
thirsty for wine.

As you arrive in our realm, know
that silence is our nature -
for it's when we chatter on
that dust and grime arrives.

---

*A reference to the practice of dampening the dirt road that led to a house, to
prevent dust from rising around honored guests as they arrived.

آب زنید راه را هین که نگار می‌رسد
مژده دهید باغ را بوی بهار می‌رسد

راه دهید یار را آن مه ده چهار را
کز رخ نوربخش او نور نثار می‌رسد

چاک شدست آسمان غلغله‌ایست در جهان
عنبر و مشک می‌دمد سنجق یار می‌رسد

رونق باغ می‌رسد چشم و چراغ می‌رسد
غم به کناره می‌رود مه به کنار می‌رسد

تیر روانه می‌رود سوی نشانه می‌رود
ما چه نشسته‌ایم پس شه ز شکار می‌رسد

باغ سلام می‌کند سرو قیام می‌کند
سبزه پیاده می‌رود غنچه سوار می‌رسد

خلوتیان آسمان تا چه شراب می‌خورند
روح خراب و مست شد عقل خمار می‌رسد

چون برسی به کوی ما خامشی است خوی ما
زآن که ز گفت و گوی ما گرد و غبار می‌رسد

{ 37 }

Now I've seen you
in your wholeness,
and so, from here on
I will not become
fragmented,
distressed;
I've seen your path,
and so, from here on
I will not travel the path
of these others.

You,
who are the king of this garden:
you feed and nurture
me, and countless more;
you satiate
my eyes, and my heart -
and so,
I will no longer be a fool
for this meager table.

Now,
Ka'beh* has come to me
and so
I will no longer travel to Ka'beh;
my moon
has come down to earth -
and so,
I will no longer aim for Saturn.

I am stout, and proud
by virtue of you;
I am bound to you,
and free by virtue of you;
I will no longer be bound
by the devil.

You rule
space and time,
hidden and evident,
like knowingness;
you are life
and the universe itself -
in your presence,
why would I not become
all spirit,
fully alive?

---

*Ka'beh - a small cube-shaped building in Mecca (Saudi Arabia) - is the focal point of the Islamic ritual pilgrimage called Hajj, and regarded by many as the house of God.

جمع تو دیدم پس از این هیچ پریشان نشوم
راه تو دیدم پس از این همره ایشان نشوم

ای که تو شاه چمنی سیرکن صد چو منی
چشم و دلم سیر کنی سخره‌ی این خوان نشوم

کعبه چو آمد سوی من جانب کعبه نروم
ماه من آمد به زمین قاصد کیوان نشوم

فربه و پرباد توام مست و خوش و شاد توام
بنده و آزاد توام بنده‌ی شیطان نشوم

شاه زمینی و زمان همچو خرد فاش و نهان
پیش تو ای جان و جهان جمله چرا جان نشوم

Published by YOUniversal Center Los Angeles, California

contact: info@youniversal.org

ALSO AVAILABLE:

THE UNIVERSE IN YOU
The first volume in the
Inner Journey series
contains 34 new
translations of Rumi,
along with the original
poems and beautiful
illustrations.
ISBN 9780692434451

THE HEART'S GARDEN
Based on a poem by Rumi.
This fully illustrated story-
book empowers kids and
adults by reminding them of
their inter-connectedness to
all and their ability to
transform the world.
Winner of the 2015
Gelett Burgess Award.
ISBN 9780692514801

CPSIA information can be obtained
at www.ICGtesting.com
Printed in the USA
LVOW13s0950260817
546484LV00028B/856/P

9 781535 510059